The True-Born Englishman by Daniel Defoe

Daniel Defoe is most well-known for his classic novels *Robinson Crusoe* and *Moll Flanders*. Born around 1660, he was also a journalist, a pamphleteer, a businessman, a spy. His life was long and colourful, and the breadth of his work, still highly regarded, is infused with similar vigour.

It is said that only the bible has been printed in more languages than Robinson Crusoe. Defoe is also noted for being one of the earliest proponents of the novel. He was extremely prolific and a very versatile writer, producing several hundred books, pamphlets, and journals on various topics including politics, crime, religion, marriage, psychology and the supernatural. He was also a pioneer of economic journalism though was made bankrupt on more on one occasion and usually mired in debt.

In later life Defoe was often most seen on Sundays when bailiffs and the like could legally make no move on him. Allegedly it was whilst hiding from creditors that he died on April 24th, 1731. He was interred in Bunhill Fields, London.

Index of Contents
AN EXPLANATORY PREFACE
PREFACE
THE INTRODUCTION
THE TRUE-BORN ENGLISHMAN
PART I
PART II
BRITANNIA
HIS FINE SPEECH, &c
THE CONCLUSION
DANIEL DEFOE – A SHORT INTRODUCTION
DANIEL DEFOE – A CONCISE BIBLIOGRAPHY

AN EXPLANATORY PREFACE

It is not that I see any reason to alter my opinion in any thing I have writ, which occasions this epistle; but I find it necessary for the satisfaction of some persons of honour, as well as wit, to pass a short explication upon it; and tell the world what I mean, or rather, what I do not mean, in some things wherein I find I am liable to be misunderstood.

I confess myself something surpris'd to hear that I am taxed with bewraying my own nest, and abusing our nation, by discovering the meanness of our original, in order to make the English contemptible abroad and at home; in which, I think, they are mistaken: for why should not our neighbours be as good as we to derive from? And I must add, that had we been an unmix'd nation, I am of opinion it had been to our disadvantage: for to go no farther, we have three nations about us as clear from mixtures of blood as any in the world, and I know not which of them I could wish ourselves to be like; I mean the

Scots, the Welsh, and the Irish; and if I were to write a reverse to the Satire, I would examine all the nations of Europe, and prove, that those nations which are most mix'd, are the best, and have least of barbarism and brutality among them; and abundance of reasons might be given for it, too long to bring into a Preface.

But I give this hint, to let the world know, that I am far from thinking, 'tis a Satire upon the English nation, to tell them, they are derived from all the nations under heaven; that is, from several nations. Nor is it meant to undervalue the original of the English, for we see no reason to like them worse, being the relicts of Romans, Danes, Saxons and Normans, than we should have done if they had remain'd Britons, that is, than if they had been all Welshmen.

But the intent of the Satire is pointed at the vanity of those who talk of their antiquity, and value themselves upon their pedigree, their ancient families, and being true-born; whereas 'tis impossible we should be true-born: and if we could, should have lost by the bargain.

These sort of people, who call themselves true-born, and tell long stories of their families, and like a nobleman of Venice, think a foreigner ought not to walk on the same side of the street with them, are own'd to be meant in this Satire. What they would infer from their long original, I know not, nor is it easy to make out whether they are the better or the worse for their ancestors: our English nation may value themselves for their wit, wealth and courage, and I believe few nations will dispute it with them; but for long originals, and ancient true-born families of English, I would advise them to wave the discourse. A true Englishman is one that deserves a character, and I have nowhere lessened him, that I know of; but as for a true-born Englishman, I confess I do not understand him.

From hence I only infer, that an Englishman, of all men, ought not to despise foreigners as such, and I think the inference is just, since what they are to-day, we were yesterday, and to-morrow they will be like us. If foreigners misbehave in their several stations and employments, I have nothing to do with that; the laws are open to punish them equally with natives, and let them have no favour.

But when I see the town full of lampoons and invectives against Dutchmen, only because they are foreigners, and the king reproached and insulted by insolent pedants, and ballad-making poets, for employing foreigners, and for being a foreigner himself, I confess myself moved by it to remind our nation of their own original, thereby to let them see what a banter is put upon ourselves in it; since speaking of Englishmen ab origine, we are really all foreigners ourselves.

I could go on to prove it is also impolitic in us to discourage foreigners; since it is easy to make it appear that the multitudes of foreign nations who have taken sanctuary here, have been the greatest additions to the wealth and strength of the nation; the essential whereof is the number of its inhabitants; nor would this nation ever have arrived to the degree of wealth and glory it now boasts of, if the addition of foreign nations, both as to manufactures and arms, had not been helpful to it. This is so plain, that he who is ignorant of it, is too dull to be talked with.

The Satire therefore I must allow to be just, till I am otherwise convinced; because nothing can be more ridiculous than to hear our people boast of that antiquity, which if it had been true, would have left us in so much worse a condition than we are in now: whereas we ought rather to boast among our neighbours, that we are part of themselves, of the same original as they, but bettered by our climate, and like our language and manufactures, derived from them, and improved by us to a perfection greater than they can pretend to.

This we might have valued ourselves upon without vanity; but to disown our descent from them, talk big of our ancient families, and long originals, and stand at a distance from foreigners, like the enthusiast in religion, with a Stand off, I am more holy than thou: this is a thing so ridiculous, in a nation derived from foreigners, as we are, that I could not but attack them as I have done.

And whereas I am threatened to be called to a public account for this freedom; and the publisher of this has been newspapered into gaol already for it; tho' I see nothing in it for which the government can be displeased; yet if at the same time those people who with an unlimited arrogance in print, every day affront the king, prescribe the parliament, and lampoon the government, may be either punished or restrained, I am content to stand and fall by the public justice of my native country, which I am not sensible I have anywhere injured.

Nor would I be misunderstood concerning the clergy; with whom, if I have taken any license more than becomes a Satire, I question not but those gentlemen, who are men of letters, are also men of so much candor, as to allow me a loose at the crimes of the guilty, without thinking the whole profession lashed who are innocent. I profess to have very mean thoughts of those gentlemen who have deserted their own principles, and exposed even their morals as well as loyalty; but not at all to think it affects any but such as are concerned in the fact.

Nor would I be misrepresented as to the ingratitude of the English to the king and his friends; as if I meant the English as a nation, are so. The contrary is so apparent, that I would hope it should not be suggested of me: and, therefore when I have brought in Britannia speaking of the king, I suppose her to be the representative or mouth of the nation, as a body. But if I say we are full of such who daily affront the king, and abuse his friends; who print scurrilous pamphlets, virulent lampoons, and reproachful public banters, against both the king's person and his government; I say nothing but what is too true; and that the Satire is directed at such, I freely own; and cannot say, but I should think it very hard to be censured for this Satire, while such remain unquestioned and tacitly approved. That I can mean none but such, is plain from these few lines, page 453. [Transcriber's Note: This reference is to a page number in the 1855 reprint edition.]

Ye heavens regard! Almighty Jove, look down, And view thy injured monarch on the throne. On their ungrateful heads due vengeance take, Who sought his aid, and then his part forsake.

If I have fallen rudely upon our vices, I hope none but the vicious will be angry. As for writing for interest, I disown it; I have neither place, nor pension, nor prospect; nor seek none, nor will have none: if matter of fact justifies the truth of the crimes, the Satire is just. As to the poetic liberties, I hope the crime is pardonable; I am content to be stoned, provided none will attack me but the innocent.

If my countrymen would take the hint, and grow better natured from my ill-natured poem as some call it; I would say this of it, that though it is far from the best Satire that ever was wrote, it would do the most good that ever Satire did.

And yet I am ready to ask pardon of some gentlemen too; who though they are Englishmen, have good nature enough to see themselves reproved, and can hear it. These are gentlemen in a true sense, that can bare to be told of their faux pas, and not abuse the reprover. To such I must say, this is no Satire; they are exceptions to the general rule; and I value my performance from their generous approbation, more than I can from any opinion I have of its worth.

The hasty errors of my verse I made my excuse for before; and since the time I have been upon it has been but little, and my leisure less, I have all along strove rather to make the thoughts explicit, than the poem correct. However, I have mended some faults in this edition, and the rest must be placed to my account.

As to answers, banters, true English Billingsgate, I expect them till nobody will buy, and then the shop will be shut. Had I wrote it for the gain of the press, I should have been concerned at its being printed again, and again, by pirates, as they call them, and paragraph-men; but would they but do it justice, and print it true, according to the copy, they are welcome to sell it for a penny, if they please.

The pence, indeed, is the end of their works. I will engage if nobody will buy, nobody will write: and not a patriot poet of them all, now will in defence of his native country, which I have abused, they say, print an answer to it, and give it about for God's sake.

PREFACE

The end of satire is reformation: and the author, though he doubt the work of conversion is at a general stop, has put his hand in the plough. I expect a storm of ill language from the fury of the town. And especially from those whose English talent it is to rail: and, without being taken for a conjuror, I may venture to foretel, that I shall be cavilled at about my mean style, rough verse, and incorrect language, things I indeed might have taken more care in. But the book is printed; and though I see some faults, it is too late to mend them. And this is all I think needful to say to them.

Possibly somebody may take me for a Dutchman; in which they are mistaken: but I am one that would be glad to see Englishmen behave themselves better to strangers, and to governors also, that one might not be reproached in foreign countries for belonging to a nation that wants manners.

I assure you, gentlemen, strangers use us better abroad; and we can give no reason but our ill-nature for the contrary here.

Methinks an Englishman who is so proud of being called a good fellow, should be civil. And it cannot be denied, but we are, in many cases, and particularly to strangers, the most churlish people alive.

As to vices, who can dispute our intemperance, while an honest drunken fellow is a character in a man's praise? All our reformations are banters, and will be so till our magistrates and gentry reform themselves, by way of example; then, and not till then, they may be expected to punish others without blushing.

As to our ingratitude, I desire to be understood of that particular people, who pretending to be Protestants, have all along endeavoured to reduce the liberties and religion of this nation into the hands of King James and his Popish powers: together with such who enjoy the peace and protection of the present government, and yet abuse and affront the king who procured it, and openly profess their uneasiness under him: these, by whatsoever names or titles they are dignified or distinguished, are the people aimed at; nor do I disown, but that it is so much the temper of an Englishman to abuse his benefactor, that I could be glad to see it rectified.

They who think I have been guilty of any error, in exposing the crimes of my own countrymen to themselves, may, among many honest instances of the like nature, find the same thing in Mr. Cowley, in his imitation of the second Olympic Ode of Pindar; his words are these:—

But in this thankless world, the givers
Are envied even by the receivers.
'Tis now the cheap and frugal fashion,
Rather to hide than pay an obligation.
Nay, 'tis much worse than so;
It now an artifice doth grow,
Wrongs and outrages they do,
Lest men should think we owe.

THE INTRODUCTION

Speak, Satire; for there's none can tell like thee
Whether 'tis folly, pride, or knavery,
That makes this discontented land appear
Less happy now in times of peace than war?
Why civil feuds disturb the nation more,
Than all our bloody wars have done before?

Fools out of favour grudge at knaves in place,
And men are always honest in disgrace:
The Court preferments make men knaves in course;
But they which would be in them would be worse.
'Tis not at foreigners that we repine,
Would foreigners their perquisites resign:
The grand contention's plainly to be seen,
To get some men put out, and some put in.
For this our Senators make long harangues,
And florid Members whet their polished tongues.
Statesmen are always sick of one disease,
And a good pension gives them present ease:
That's the specific makes them all content
With any King and any Government.
Good patriots at Court abuses rail,
And all the nation's grievances bewail;
But when the sovereign balsam's once applied,
The zealot never fails to change his side;
And when he must the golden key resign,
The railing spirit comes about again.

Who shall this bubbled nation disabuse,
While they their own felicities refuse,

Who at the wars have made such mighty pother,
And now are falling out with one another:
With needless fears the jealous nation fill,
And always have been saved against their will:
Who fifty millions sterling have disbursed,
To be with peace and too much plenty cursed:
Who their old monarch eagerly undo,
And yet uneasily obey the new.
Search, Satire, search: a deep incision make;
The poison's strong, the antidote's too weak.
'Tis pointed truth must manage this dispute,
And downright English, Englishmen confute.

Whet thy just anger at the nation's pride,
And with keen phrase repel the vicious tide;
To Englishmen their own beginnings show,
And ask them why they slight their neighbours so.
Go back to elder times and ages past,
And nations into long oblivion cast;
To old Britannia's youthful days retire,
And there for true-born Englishmen inquire.
Britannia freely will disown the name,
And hardly knows herself from whence they came:
Wonders that they of all men should pretend
To birth and blood, and for a name contend.
Go back to causes where our follies dwell,
And fetch the dark original from hell:
Speak, Satire, for there's none like thee can tell.

THE TRUE-BORN ENGLISHMAN

PART I

Wherever God erects a house of prayer,
The Devil always builds a chapel there:[1]
And 'twill be found upon examination,
The latter has the largest congregation:
For ever since he first debauched the mind,
He made a perfect conquest of mankind.
With uniformity of service, he
Reigns with a general aristocracy.
No non-conforming sects disturb his reign,
For of his yoke there's very few complain.
He knows the genius and the inclination,
And matches proper sins for every nation.
He needs no standing-army government;

He always rules us by our own consent:
His laws are easy, and his gentle sway
Makes it exceeding pleasant to obey:
The list of his vicegerents and commanders,
Outdoes your Cæsars or your Alexanders.

[1] This old proverb was quoted by Robert Burton in his "Anatomy of Melancholy" (1621), "Where God hath a temple the Devil hath a chapel" (Part III. sc. iv. subs. I). It was also No. 670 in George Herbert's "Jacula Prudentium," first published in 1640, where it ran, "No sooner is a temple built to God but the Devil builds a chapel hard by." Defoe was the first rhymer of the proverb, and the rider to it is his own.

They never fail of his infernal aid,
And he's as certain ne'er to be betrayed.
Through all the world they spread his vast command,
And Death's eternal empire is maintained.
They rule so politicly and so well,
As if they were Lords Justices of Hell,
Duly divided to debauch mankind,
And plant infernal dictates in his mind.

Pride, the first peer, and president of Hell,
To his share Spain, the largest province, fell.
The subtile Prince thought fittest to bestow
On these the golden mines of Mexico,
With all the silver mountains of Peru,
Wealth which would in wise hands the world undo:
Because he knew their genius was such,
Too lazy and too haughty to be rich.
So proud a people, so above their fate,
That if reduced to beg, they'll beg in state;
Lavish of money to be counted brave,
And proudly starve because they scorn to save.
Never was nation in the world before
So very rich and yet so very poor.

Lust chose the torrid zone of Italy,
Where blood ferments in rapes and sodomy:
Where swelling veins o'erflow with livid streams,
With heat impregnate from Vesuvian flames:
Whose flowing sulphur forms infernal lakes,
And human body of the soil partakes.
There nature ever burns with hot desires,
Fann'd with luxuriant air from subterranean fires;
Here, undisturbed in floods of scalding lust,
The Infernal King reigns with infernal gust.

Drunkenness, the darling favourite of Hell,

Chose Germany to rule; and rules so well,
No subjects more obsequiously obey,
None please so well or are so pleased as they.
The cunning artist manages so well,
He lets them bow to Heaven and drink to Hell.
If but to wine and him they homage pay,
He cares not to what deity they pray,
What god they worship most, or in what way.
Whether by Luther, Calvin, or by Rome
They sail for Heaven, by Wine he steers them home.

Ungoverned Passion settled first in France,
Where mankind lives in haste and thrives by chance;
A dancing nation, fickle and untrue,
Have oft undone themselves and others too;
Prompt the infernal dictates to obey,
And in Hell's favour none more great than they.

The Pagan world he blindly leads away,
And personally rules with arbitrary sway;
The mask thrown off, plain Devil his title stands,
And what elsewhere he tempts he there commands,
There with full gust the ambition of his mind
Governs, as he of old in Heaven designed.
Worshipped as God, his Paynim altars smoke,
Embrued with blood of those that him invoke.

The rest by Deputies he rules as well,
And plants the distant colonies of Hell.
By them his secret power he maintains,
And binds the world in his infernal chains.

By Zeal the Irish, and the Russ by Folly:
Fury the Dane, The Swede by Melancholy;
By stupid Ignorance the Muscovite;
The Chinese by a child of Hell called Wit.
Wealth makes the Persian too effeminate,
And Poverty the Tartars desperate;
The Turks and Moors by Mah'met he subdues,
And God has given him leave to rule the Jews.
Rage rules the Portuguese and Fraud the Scotch,
Revenge the Pole and Avarice the Dutch.

Satire, be kind, and draw a silent veil
Thy native England's vices to conceal;
Or, if that task's impossible to do,
At least be just, and show her virtues too—
Too great the first; alas, the last too few!

England, unknown as yet, unpeopled lay;
Happy had she remained so to this day,
And not to every nation been a prey.
Her open harbours and her fertile plains
(The merchant's glory those, and these the swain's)
To every barbarous nation have betrayed her,
Who conquer her as oft as they invade her;
So beauty's guarded but by innocence,
That ruins her, which should be her defence.

Ingratitude, a devil of black renown,
Possessed her very early for his own.
An ugly, surly, sullen, selfish spirit,
Who Satan's worst perfections does inherit;
Second to him in malice and in force,
All devil without, and all within him worse. .

He made her first-born race to be so rude,
And suffered her so oft to be subdued;
By several crowds of wandering thieves o'errun,
Often unpeopled, and as oft undone;
While every nation that her powers reduced
Their languages and manners introduced.
From whose mixed relics our compounded breed
By spurious generation does succeed,
Making a race uncertain and uneven,
Derived from all the nations under Heaven.

The Romans first with Julius Cæsar came,
Including all the nations of that name,
Gauls, Greeks, and Lombards, and, by computation,
Auxiliaries or slaves of every nation.
With Hengist, Saxons; Danes with Sueno came,
In search of plunder, not in search of fame.
Scots, Picts, and Irish from the Hibernian shore,
And conquering William brought the Normans o'er.

All these their barbarous offspring left behind,
The dregs of armies, they of all mankind;
Blended with Britons, who before were here,
Of whom the Welsh ha' blessed the character.

From this amphibious ill-born mob began
That vain ill-natured thing, an Englishman.
The customs, surnames, languages, and manners
Of all these nations are their own explainers:
Whose relics are so lasting and so strong,

They ha' left a shibboleth upon our tongue,
By which with easy search you may distinguish
Your Roman-Saxon-Danish-Norman English.

The great invading Norman[1] let us know
What conquerors in after-times might do.
To every musketeer[2] he brought to town,
He gave the lands which never were his own.
When first the English crown he did obtain,
He did not send his Dutchmen back again.
No reassumptions in his reign were known,
D'Avenant might there ha' let his book alone.
No Parliament his army could disband;
He raised no money, for he paid in land.
He gave his legions their eternal station,
And made them all freeholders of the nation.
He cantoned out the country to his men,
And every soldier was a denizen.
The rascals thus enriched, he called them lords,
To please their upstart pride with new-made words,
And Doomsday Book his tyranny records.

[1] William the Conqueror. [D.F.]
[2] Or archer. [D.F.]

And here begins our ancient pedigree,
That so exalts our poor nobility:
'Tis that from some French trooper they derive,
Who with the Norman bastard did arrive;

The trophies of the families appear,
Some show the sword, the bow, and some the spear,
Which their great ancestor, forsooth, did wear.
These in the herald's register remain,
Their noble mean extraction to explain,
Yet who the hero was, no man can tell,
Whether a drummer or a colonel:
The silent record blushes to reveal
Their undescended dark original.

But grant the best, how came the change to pass,
A true-born Englishman of Norman race?
A Turkish horse can show more history,
To prove his well-descended family.
Conquest, as by the moderns[1] it is expressed,
May give a title to the lands possessed:
But that the longest sword should be so civil
To make a Frenchman English, that's the devil.

[1] Dr. Sherlock, de facto. [D.F.]

These are the heroes that despise the Dutch,
And rail at new-come foreigners so much,
Forgetting that themselves are all derived
From the most scoundrel race that ever lived;
A horrid crowd of rambling thieves and drones,
Who ransacked kingdoms and dispeopled towns,
The Pict and painted Briton, treacherous Scot,
By hunger, theft, and rapine hither brought;
Norwegian pirates, buccaneering Danes,
Whose red-haired offspring everywhere remains,
Who, joined with Norman-French, compound the breed
From whence your true-born Englishmen proceed.

And lest by Length of time it be pretended
The climate may this modern breed ha' mended,
Wise Providence, to keep us where we are,
Mixes us daily with exceeding care.
We have been Europe's sink, the jakes where she
Voids all her offal outcast progeny.

From our eighth Henry's time, the strolling bands
Of banished fugitives from neighboring lands
Have here a certain sanctuary found:
The eternal refuge of the vagabond,
Where, in but half a common age of time,
Borrowing new blood and manners from the clime,
Proudly they learn all mankind to contemn,
And all their race are true-born Englishmen.

Dutch, Walloons, Flemings, Irishmen, and Scots,
Vaudois and Valtelins, and Hugonots,
In good Queen Bess's charitable reign,
Supplied us with three hundred thousand men.
Religion—God, we thank Thee!—sent them hither,
Priests, Protestants, the Devil and all together:
Of all professions and of every trade,
All that were persecuted or afraid;
Whether for debt or other crimes they fled,
David at Hachilah was still their head.

The offspring of this miscellaneous crowd
Had not their new plantations long enjoyed,
But they grew Englishmen, and raised their votes
At foreign shoals for interloping Scots.
The royal branch[1] from Pictland did succeed,

With troops of Scots and Scabs from North-by-Tweed.
The seven first years of his pacific reign
Made him and half his nation Englishmen.
Scots from the northern frozen banks of Tay,
With packs and plods came whigging all away:
Thick as the locusts which in Egypt swarmed,
With pride and hungry hopes completely armed;
With native truth, diseases, and no money,
Plundered our Canaan of the milk and honey.
Here they grew quickly lords and gentlemen,
And all their race are true-born Englishmen.

[1] K. J. I. [D.F.]

The civil wars, the common purgative,
Which always use to make the nation thrive,
Made way for all that strolling congregation,
Which thronged in Pious Charles's restoration.[1]
The royal refugee our breed restores,
With foreign courtiers and with foreign whores,
And carefully repeopled us again,
Throughout his lazy, long, lascivious reign;
With such a blest and true-born English fry,
As much illustrates our nobility.
A gratitude which will so black appear,
As future ages must abhor to hear,
When they look back on all that crimson flood,
Which streamed in Lindsay's, and Carnarvon's blood,
Bold Strafford, Cambridge, Capel, Lucas, Lisle,
Who crowned in death his father's funeral pile.
The loss of whom, in order to supply,
With true-born-English nationality,
Six bastard Dukes survive his luscious reign,
The labours of Italian Castlemaine,[2]
French Portsmouth,[3] Tabby Scot, and Cambrian.
Besides the numerous bright and virgin throng,
Whole female glories shade them from my song.

[1] K. C. II. [D.F.]

[2] *Lady Castlemaine, of the Italian-French family of Villars, was first known to Charles II. as Mrs. Palmer. Afterwards her husband was made Earl of Castlemaine, and in 1668 she was made Duchess of Cleveland. Of the cost of this woman Andrew Marvell wrote:*—*"They have signed and sealed ten thousand pounds a year more to the Duchess of Cleveland; who has likewise near ten thousand pounds a year out of the new farm of the country excise of beer and ale; five thousand pounds a year out of the Post Office; and, they say, the reversion of all the King's leases, the reversion of all places in the Custom House, the green-wax, and, indeed, what not? All promotions, spiritual and temporal, pass under her cognisance," &c. Charles II. had by her five children.*

[3] Louise Renée de Puencovet de Queroualle came over to Dover as a maid of honour, and was created Duchess of Portsmouth in August 1673. She cost as much as Lady Castlemaine. Her son, Charles Lennox, was made Duke of Richmond. The Duchess of Portsmouth was living when this satire appeared. She died in 1734.

This offspring, if one age they multiply,
May half the house with English peers supply;
There with true English pride they may contemn
Schomberg and Portland,[1] new made noblemen.

[1] Frederick de Schomberg, an old favourite of King William's, was made Duke of Schomberg on the 10th of April 1689. Another friend of the King's, William Bentinck, was created Earl of Portland on the 9th of April 1689. His son and heir was raised to a dukedom in 1716.

French cooks, Scotch pedlars, and Italian whores,
Were all made lords, or lords' progenitors.
Beggars and bastards by his new creation
Much multiplied the peerage of the nation;
Who will be all, ere one short age runs o'er,
As true-born lords as those we had before.

Then to recruit the Commons he prepares
And heal the latent breaches of the wars;
The pious purpose better to advance,
He invites the banished Protestants of France:
Hither for God's sake and their own they fled,
Some for religion came, and some for bread;
Two hundred thousand pair of wooden shoes,
Who, God be thanked, had nothing left to lose,
To Heaven's great praise did for religion fly,
To make us starve our poor in charity.
In every port they plant their fruitful train,
To get a race of true-born Englishmen;
Whose children will, when riper years they see,
Be as ill-natured and as proud as we;
Call themselves English, foreigners despise,
Be surly like us all, and just as wise.

Thus from a mixture of all kinds began,
That heterogeneous thing an Englishman;
In eager rapes and furious lust begot,
Betwixt a painted Briton and a Scot;
Whose gendering offspring quickly learned to bow,
And yoke their heifers to the Roman plough;
From whence a mongrel half-bred race there came,
With neither name nor nation, speech nor fame;
In whose hot veins new mixtures quickly ran,

Infused betwixt a Saxon and a Dane;
While their rank daughters, to their parents just,
Received all nations with promiscuous lust.
This nauseous brood directly did contain
The well-extracted brood of Englishmen.

Which medley cantoned in a Heptarchy,
A rhapsody of nations to supply,
Among themselves maintained eternal wars,
And still the ladies loved the conquerors.

The Western Angles all the rest subdued,
A bloody nation, barbarous and rude,
Who by the tenure of the sword possessed
One part of Britain, and subdued the rest.
And as great things denominate the small,
The conquering part gave title to the whole;
The Scot, Pict, Briton, Roman, Dane, submit,
And with the English-Saxon all unite;
And these the mixtures have so close pursued,
The very name and memory's subdued.
No Roman now, no Briton does remain;
Wales strove to separate, but strove in vain;
The silent nations undistinguished fall,
And Englishman's the common name of all.
Fate jumbled them together, God knows how;
Whate'er they were, they're true-born English now.

The wonder which remains is at our pride,
To value that which all wise men deride.
For Englishmen to boast of generation
Cancels their knowledge and lampoons the nation.
A true-born Englishman's a contradiction,
In speech an irony, in fact a fiction;
A banter made to be a test of fools,
Which those that use it justly ridicules;
A metaphor invented to express
A man akin to all the universe.

For, as the Scots, as learned men have said,
Throughout the world their wandering seed have spread;
So open-handed England, 'tis believed,
Has all the gleanings of the world received.

Some think of England 'twas our Saviour meant,
The Gospel should to all the world be sent,
Since, when the blessed sound did hither reach,
They to all nations might be said to preach.

'Tis well that virtue gives nobility,
How shall we else the want of birth and blood supply?
Since scarce one family is left alive
Which does not from some foreigner derive.
Of sixty thousand English gentlemen,
Whose names and arms in registers remain,
We challenge all our heralds to declare
Ten families which English-Saxons are.

France justly owns the ancient noble line
Of Bourbon, Montmorency, and Lorraine,
The Germans too their House of Austria show
And Holland their invincible Nassau,
Lines which in heraldry were ancient grown
Before the name of Englishman was known.
Even Scotland, too, her elder glory shows,
Her Gordons, Hamiltons, and her Monros,
Douglas, Mackays, and Grahams, names well known
Long before ancient England knew her own.

But England, modern to the last degree,
Borrows or makes her own nobility,
And yet she boldly boasts of pedigree;
Repines that foreigners are put upon her,
And talks of her antiquity and honour;
Her Sackvilles, Saviles, Capels, De la Meres,
Mohuns, and Montagues, Darcys, and Veres,
Not one have English names, yet all are English peers.
Your Hermans, Papillons, and Lavalliers,
Pass now for true-born English knights and squires,
And make good senate members or Lord Mayors.
Wealth, howsoever got, in England makes
Lords of mechanics, gentlemen of rakes:
Antiquity and birth are needless here;
'Tis impudence and money makes a peer.

Innumerable City knights, we know,
From Bluecoat Hospital and Bridewell flow.
Draymen and porters fill the city Chair,
And footboys magisterial purple wear.
Fate has but very small distinction set
Betwixt the counter and the coronet.
Tarpaulin lords, pages of high renown,
Rise up by poor men's valour, not their own.
Great families of yesterday we show,
And lords, whose parents were the Lord knows who.

PART II

The breed's described: Now, Satire, if you can,
Their temper show, for manners make the man.
Fierce, as the Briton; as the Roman, brave;
And less inclined to conquer than to save;
Eager to fight, and lavish of their blood,
And equally of fear and forecast void.
The Pict has made 'em sour, the Dane morose;
False from the Scot, and from the Norman worse.
What honesty they have, the Saxons gave them,
And that, now they grow old, begins to leave them.
The climate makes them terrible and bold,
And English beef their courage does uphold;
No danger can their daring spirit pall,
Always provided that their belly's full.

In close intrigues their faculty's but weak,
For generally whate'er they know they speak,
And often their own counsels undermine
By their infirmity, and not design;
From whence the learned say it does proceed,
That English treasons never can succeed;
For they're so open-hearted, you may know
Their own most secret thoughts, and others too.

The lab'ring poor, in spite of double pay,
Are saucy, mutinous, and beggarly,
So lavish of their money and their time,
That want of forecast is the nation's crime.
Good drunken company is their delight,
And what they get by day they spend by night.
Dull thinking seldom does their heads engage,
But drink their youth away, and hurry on old age.
Empty of all good husbandry and sense,
And void of manners most when void of pence.
Their strong aversion to behaviour's such,
They always talk too little or too much;
So dull, they never take the pains to think,
And seldom are good-natured, but in drink.

In English ale their dear enjoyment lies,
For which they'll starve themselves and families.
An Englishman will fairly drink as much
As will maintain two families of Dutch:
Subjecting all their labour to their pots;

The greatest artists are the greatest sots.

The country poor do by example live,
The gentry lead them, and the clergy drive:
What may we not from such examples hope?
The landlord is their god, the priest their pope.
A drunken clergy and a swearing bench
Has given the Reformation such a drench,
As wise men think there is some cause to doubt
Will purge good manners and religion out.

Nor do the poor alone their liquor prize;
The sages join in this great sacrifice;
The learned men who study Aristotle,
Correct him with an explanation bottle;
Praise Epicurus rather than Lysander,
And Aristippus[1] more than Alexander.
The doctors, too ,their Galen here resign,
And generally prescribe specific wine;
The graduate's study's grown an easier task,
While for the urinal they toss the flask;
The surgeon's art grows plainer every hour,
And wine's the balm which into wounds they pour;

[1] *The drunkard's name for Canary.* [D.F.]

Poets long since Parnassus have forsaken,
And say the ancient bards were all mistaken.
Apollo's lately abdicate and fled,
And good King Bacchus governs in his stead;
He does the chaos of the head refine,
And atom-thoughts jump into words by wine:
The inspirations of a finer nature,
As wine must needs excel Parnassus' water.

Statesmen their weighty politics refine,
And soldiers raise their courages by wine;
Cecilia gives her choristers their choice,
And let's them all drink wine to clear their voice.
Some think the clergy first found out the way,
And wine's the only spirit by which they pray;
But others, less profane than so, agree
It clears the lungs and helps the memory;
And therefore all of them divinely think,
Instead of study, 'tis as well to drink.

And here I would be very glad to know
Whether our Asgilites may drink or no;

Th' englight'ning fumes of wine would certainly
Assist them much when they begin to fly;
Or if a fiery chariot should appear,
Inflamed by wine, they'd have the less to fear.

Even the gods themselves, as mortals say,
Were they on earth, would be as drunk as they;
Nectar would be no more celestial drink,
They'd all take wine, to teach them how to think.
But English drunkards gods and men outdo,
Drink their estates away, and money too.
Colon's in debt, and if his friends should fail
To help him out, must die at last in gaol;
His wealthy uncle sent a hundred nobles,
To pay his trifles off, and rid him of his troubles;
But Colon, like a true-born Englishman,
Drank all the money out in bright champagne,
And Colon does in custody remain.
Drunk'ness has been the darling of the realm,
E'er since a drunken pilot bad the helm.

In their religion they are so uneven,
That each man goes his own by-way to Heaven.
Tenacious of mistakes to that degree
That ev'ry man pursues it sep'rately,
And fancies none can find the way but he:
So shy of one another they are grown,
As if they strove to get to Heaven alone.
Rigid and zealous, positive and grave,
And ev'ry grace but Charity they have.
This makes them so ill-natured and uncivil,
That all men think an Englishman the devil.

Surly to strangers, froward to their friend;
Submit to love with a reluctant mind.
Resolved to be ungrateful and unkind,
If by necessity reduced to ask,
The giver has the difficultest task;
For what's bestowed they awkwardly receive,
And always take less freely than they give.
The obligation is their highest grief,
And never love where they accept relief.
So sullen in their sorrow, that 'tis known,
They'll rather die than their afflictions own;
And if relieved, it is too often true
That they'll abuse their benefactors too;
For in distress, their haughty stomach's such,
They hate to see themselves obliged too much.

Seldom contented, often in the wrong,
Hard to be pleased at all, and never long.

If your mistakes their ill opinion gain,
No merit can their favour re-obtain;
And if they're not vindictive in their fury,
'Tis their unconstant temper does secure ye.
Their brain's so cool, their passion seldom burns,
For all's condensed before the flame returns;
The fermentation's of so weak a matter,
The humid damps the fume, and runs it all to water.
So, though the inclination may be strong,
They're pleased by fits, and never angry long.

Then, if good-nature shows some slender proof,
They never think they have reward enough,
But like our modern Quakers of the town,
Expect your manners, and return you none.

Friendship, th' abstracted union of the mind,
Which all men seek, but very few can find:
Of all the nations in the universe,
None talk on't more, or understand it less;
For if it does their property annoy,
Their property their friendship will destroy.

As you discourse them, you shall hear them tell
All things in which they think they do excel.
No panegyric needs their praise record;
An Englishman ne'er wants his own good word.
His long discourses gen'rally appear
Prologued with his own wond'rous character.
But first to illustrate his own good name,
He never fails his neighbour to defame;
And yet he really designs no wrong—
His malice goes no further than his tongue.
But pleased to tattle, he delights to rail,
To satisfy the lech'ry of a tale.
His own dear praises close the ample speech;
Tells you how wise he is—that is, how rich:
For wealth is wisdom; he that's rich is wise;
And all men learnéd poverty despise.
His generosity comes next, and then
Concludes that he's a true-born Englishman;
And they, 'tis known, are generous and free,
Forgetting and forgiving injury:
Which may be true, thus rightly understood,
Forgiving ill turns, and forgetting good.

Cheerful in labour when they've undertook it,
But out of humour, when they're out of pocket.
But if their belly and their pocket's full,
They may be phlegmatic, but never dull:
And if a bottle does their brains refine,
It makes their wit as sparkling as their wine.

As for the general vices which we find
They're guilty of, in common with mankind,
Satire, forbear, and silently endure;
We must conceal the crimes we cannot cure.
Nor shall my verse the brighter sex defame,
For English beauty will preserve her name,
Beyond dispute, agreeable and fair,
And modester than other nations are:
For where the vice prevails, the great temptation
Is want of money more than inclination.
In general, this only is allowed,
They're something noisy, and a little proud.

An Englishman is gentlest in command,
Obedience is a stranger in the land:
Hardly subjected to the magistrate;
For Englishmen do all subjection hate.
Humblest when rich, but peevish when they're poor,
And think, whate'er they have, they merit more.

The meanest English ploughman studies law,
And keeps thereby the magistrates in awe;
Will boldly tell them what they ought to do,
And sometimes punish their omissions too.

Their liberty and property's so dear,
They scorn their laws or governors to fear:
So bugbeared with the name of slavery,
They can't submit to their own liberty.
Restraint from ill is freedom to the wise;
But Englishmen do all restraint despise.
Slaves to the liquor, drudges to the pots,
The mob are statesmen and their statesmen sots.

Their governors they count such dangerous things,
That 'tis their custom to affront their kings:
So jealous of the power their kings possest,
They suffer neither power nor king to rest.
The bad with force they eagerly subdue:
The good with constant clamours they pursue;

And did King Jesus reign, they'd murmur too.
A discontented nation, and by far
Harder to rule in times of peace than war:
Easily set together by the ears,
And full of causeless jealousies and fears:
Apt to revolt, and willing to rebel,
And never are contented when they're well.
No Government could ever please them long,
Could tie their hands, or rectify their tongue:
In this to ancient Israel well compared,
Eternal murmurs are among them heard.

It was but lately that they were oppressed,
Their rights invaded, and their laws suppressed:
When nicely tender of their liberty,
Lord! what a noise they made of slavery.
In daily tumult show'd their discontent,
Lampooned the King, and mocked his Government.

And if in arms they did not first appear,
'Twas want of force, and not for want of fear.
In humbler tone than English used to do,
At foreign hands for foreign aid they sue.

William, the great successor of Nassau,
Their prayers heard and their oppressions saw:
He saw and saved them; God and him they praised,
To this their thanks, to that their trophies raised.
But, glutted with their own felicities,
They soon their new deliverer despise;
Say all their prayers back, their joy disown,
Unsing their thanks, and pull their trophies down;
Their harps of praise are on the willows hung,
For Englishmen are ne'er contented long.

The reverend clergy, too! Who would have thought
That they, who had such non-resistance taught,
Should e'er to arms against their prince be brought,
Who up to Heaven did regal power advance,
Subjecting English laws to modes of France,
Twisting religion so with loyalty,
As one could never live and t'other die.
And yet no sooner did their prince design
Their glebes and perquisites to undermine,
But, all their passive doctrines laid aside,
The clergy their own principles denied;
Unpreached their non-resisting cant, and prayed
To Heaven for help and to the Dutch for aid.

The Church chimed all her doctrines back again,
And pulpit champions did the cause maintain;
Flew in the face of all their former zeal,
And non-resistance did at once repeal.

The Rabbis say it would be too prolix,
To tie religion up to politics:
The Church's safety is suprema lex.
And so, by a new figure of their own,
Their former doctrines all at once disown;
As laws post facto in the Parliament
In urgent cases have obtained assent,
But are as dangerous precedents laid by,
Made lawful only by necessity.

The reverend fathers then in arms appear,
And men of God become the men of war.
The nation, fired by them, to arms apply,
Assault their Antichristian monarchy;
To their due channel all our laws restore,
And made things what they should have been before.
But when they came to fill the vacant throne,
And the pale priests looked back on what they'd done;
How English liberty began to thrive,
And Church of England loyalty outlive;
How all their persecuting days were done,
And their deliverer placed upon the throne:
The priests, as priests are wont to do, turned tail;
They're Englishmen, and nature will prevail.
Now they deplore the ruins they have made,
And murmur for the master they betrayed,
Excuse those crimes they could not make him mend;
And suffer for the cause they can't defend.
Pretend they'd not have carried things so high,
And proto-martyrs make for Popery.
Had the prince done as they designed the thing,
Have set the clergy up to rule the King,
Taken a donative for coming hither,
And so have left their King and them together,
We had, say they, been now a happy nation.
No doubt we had seen a blessed reformation:
For wise men say 't's as dangerous a thing,
A ruling priesthood as a priest-rid king;
And of all plagues with which mankind are curst,
Ecclesiastic tyranny's the worst.

If all our former grievances were feigned,
King James has been abused and we trepanned;

Bugbeared with Popery and power despotic,
Tyrannic goverment and leagues exotic:
The Revolution's a fanatic plot,
William a tyrant, Sunderland a sot:
A factious army and a poisoned nation
Unjustly forced King James's abdication.

But if he did the subjects' rights invade,
Then he was punished only, not betrayed;
And punishing of kings is no such crime,
But Englishmen have done it many a time.

When kings the sword of justice first lay down,
They are no kings, though they possess the crown:
Titles are shadows, crowns are empty things,
The good of subjects is the end of kings;
To guide in war and to protect in peace;
Where tyrants once commence the kings do cease;
For arbitrary power's so strange a thing,
It makes the tyrant and unmakes the king.

If kings by foreign priests and armies reign,
And lawless power against their oaths maintain,
Then subjects must have reason to complain.
If oaths must bind us when our kings do ill,
To call in foreign aid is to rebel.
By force to circumscribe our lawful prince
Is wilful treason in the largest sense;
And they who once rebel, most certainly
Their God, and king, and former oaths defy.
If we allow no mal-administration
Could cancel the allegiance of the nation,
Let all our learned sons of Levi try
This ecclesastic riddle to untie:
How they could make a step to call the prince,
And yet pretend to oaths and innocence?

By the first address they made beyond the seas,
They're perjured in the most intense degrees;
And without scruple for the time to come
May swear to all the kings in Christendom.
And truly did our kings consider all,
They'd never let the clergy swear at all;
Their politic allegiance they'd refuse,
For whores and priests will never want excuse.

But if the mutual contract were dissolved,
The doubts explained, the difficulty solved,

That kings, when they descend to tyranny,
Dissolve the bond and leave the subject free.
The government's ungirt when justice dies,
And constitutions are non-entities;
The nation's all a Mob, there's no such thing
As Lords or Commons, Parliament or King.
A great promiscuous crowd the hydra lies
Till laws revive and mutual contract ties;
A chaos free to choose for their own share
What case of government they please to wear.
If to a king they do the reins commit,
All men are bound in conscience to submit;
But then that king must by his oath assent
To postulatas of the government,
Which if he breaks, he cuts off the entail,
And power retreats to its original.

This doctrine has the sanction of assent,
From Nature's universal Parliament.
The voice of Nature and the course of things
Allow that laws superior are to kings.
None but delinquents would have justice cease;
Knaves rail at laws as soldiers rail at peace;
For justice is the end of government,
As reason is the test of argument.

No man was ever yet so void of sense
As to debate the right of self-defence,
A principle so grafted in the mind,
With Nature born, and does like Nature bind;
Twisted with reason and with Nature too,
As neither one or other can undo.

Nor can this right be less when national;
Reason, which governs one, should govern all.
Whate'er the dialects of courts may tell,
He that his right demands can ne'er rebel,
Which right, if 'tis by governors denied,
May be procured by force or foreign aid;
For tyranny's a nation's term of grief,
As folks cry "Fire" to hasten in relief;
And when the hated word is heard about,
All men should come to help the people out.

Thus England groaned—Britannia's voice was heard,
And great Nassau to rescue her appeared,
Called by the universal voice of Fate—
God and the people's legal magistrate.

Ye Heavens regard! Almighty Jove look down,
And view thy injured monarch on the throne.
On their ungrateful heads due vengeance take,
Who sought his aid and then his part forsake.
Witness, ye Powers! It was our call alone,
Which now our pride makes us ashamed to own.
Britannia's troubles fetched him from afar,
To court the dreadful casualties of war;
But where requital never can be made,
Acknowledgment's a tribute seldom paid.

He dwelt in bright Maria's circling arms,
Defended by the magic of her charms,
From foreign fears and from domestic harms.
Ambition found no fuel to her fire;
He had what God could give or man desire.
Till pity roused him from his soft repose,
His life to unseen hazards to expose;
Till pity moved him in our cause t' appear;
Pity! that word which now we hate to hear.
But English gratitude is always such,
To hate the hand which doth oblige too much.

Britannia's cries gave birth to his intent,
And hardly gained his unforeseen assent;
His boding thoughts foretold him he should find
The people fickle, selfish, and unkind.
Which thought did to his royal heart appear
More dreadful than the dangers of the war;
For nothing grates a generous mind so soon
As base returns for hearty service done.

Satire, be silent! awfully prepare
Britannia's song and William's praise to hear.
Stand by, and let her cheerfully rehearse
Her grateful vows in her immortal verse.
Loud Fame's eternal trumpet let her sound;
Listen, ye distant Poles and endless round.
May the strong blast the welcome news convey
As far as sound can reach or spirit can fly.
To neighb'ring worlds, if such there be, relate
Our hero's fame, for theirs to imitate.
To distant worlds of spirits let her rehearse:
For spirits, without the help of voice, converse.
May angels hear the gladsome news on high,
Mixed with their everlasting symphony.
And Hell itself stand in suspense to know
Whether it be the fatal blast or no.

BRITANNIA

The fame of virtue 'tis for which I sound,
And heroes with immortal triumphs crowned.
Fame, built on solid virtue, swifter flies
Than morning light can spread my eastern skies.
The gath'ring air returns the doubling sound,
And loud repeating thunders force it round;
Echoes return from caverns of the deep;
Old Chaos dreams on't in eternal sleep;
Time hands it forward to its latest urn,
From whence it never, never shall return;
Nothing is heard so far or lasts so long;
'Tis heard by every ear and spoke by every tongue.
My hero, with the sails of honour furled,
Rises like the great genius of the world.
By Fate and Fame wisely prepared to be
The soul of war and life of victory;
He spreads the wings of virtue on the throne,
And every wind of glory fans them on.
Immortal trophies dwell upon his brow,
Fresh as the garlands he has won but now.

By different steps the high ascent he gains,
And differently that high ascent maintains.
Princes for pride and lust of rule make war,
And struggle for the name of conqueror.
Some fight for fame, and some for victory;
He fights to save, and conquers to set free.

Then seek no phrase his titles to conceal,
And hide with words what actions must reveal.
No parallel from Hebrew stories take
Of god-like kings my similies to make;
No borrowed names conceal my living theme,
But names and things directly I proclaim.
'Tis honest merit does his glory raise,
Whom that exalts let no man fear to praise:
Of such a subject no man need be shy,
Virtue's above the reach of flattery.
He needs no character but his own fame,
Nor any flattering titles but his name:
William's the name that's spoke by every tongue,
William's the darling subject of my song.
Listen, ye virgins to the charming sound,

And in eternal dances hand it round:
Your early offerings to this altar bring,
Make him at once a lover and a king.
May be submit to none but to your arms,
Nor ever be subdued but by your charms.
May your soft thoughts for him be all sublime,
And every tender vow be made for him.
May he be first in every morning thought,
And Heaven ne'er hear a prayer when he's left out.
May every omen, every boding dream,
Be fortunate by mentioning his name;
May this one charm infernal power affright,
And guard you from the terrors of the night;
May every cheerful glass, as it goes down
To William's health, be cordials to your own.
Let every song be chorused with his name,
And music pay her tribute to his fame;
Let every poet tune his artful verse,
And in immortal strains his deeds rehearse.
And may Apollo never more inspire
The disobedient bard with his seraphic fire;
May all my sons their grateful homage pay,
His praises sing, and for his safety pray.

Satire, return to our unthankful isle,
Secured by Heaven's regard and William's toil;
To both ungrateful and to both untrue,
Rebels to God, and to good-nature too.

If e'er this nation be distressed again,
To whomsoe'er they cry, they'll cry in vain;
To Heaven they cannot have the face to look,
Or, if they should, it would but Heaven provoke.
To hope for help from man would be too much,
Mankind would always tell them of the Dutch;
How they came here our freedoms to obtain,
Were paid and cursed, and hurried home again;
How by their aid we first dissolved our fears,
And then our helpers damned for foreigners.
'Tis not our English temper to do better,
For Englishmen think every man their debtor.

'Tis worth observing that we ne'er complained
Of foreigners, nor of the wealth they gained,
Till all their services were at an end.
Wise men affirm it is the English way
Never to grumble till they come to pay,
And then they always think, their temper's such,

The work too little and the pay too much.
As frightened patients, when they want a cure,
Bid any price, and any pain endure;
But when the doctor's remedies appear,
The cure's too easy and the price too dear.

Great Portland ne'er was bantered when he strove
For us his master's kindest thoughts to move;
We ne'er lampooned his conduct when employed
King James's secret counsels to divide:
Then we caressed him as the only man
Which could the doubtful oracle explain;
The only Hushai able to repel
The dark designs of our Achitophel;
Compared his master's courage to his sense,
The ablest statesman and the bravest prince.
On his wise conduct we depended much,
And liked him ne'er the worse for being Dutch.
Nor was he valued more than he deserved,
Freely he ventured, faithfully he served.
In all King William's dangers he has shared;
In England's quarrels always he appeared:
The Revolution first, and then the Boyne,
In both his counsels and his conduct shine;
His martial valour Flanders will confess,
And France regrets his managing the peace.
Faithful to England's interest and her king;
The greatest reason of our murmuring.
Ten years in English service he appeared,
And gained his master's and the world's regard:
But 'tis not England's custom to reward.
The wars are over, England needs him not;
Now he's a Dutchman, and the Lord knows what.

Schomberg, the ablest soldier of his age,
With great Nassau did in our cause engage:
Both joined for England's rescue and defence,
The greatest captain and the greatest prince.
With what applause his stories did we tell!
Stories which Europe's volumes largely swell.
We counted him an army in our aid:
Where he commanded, no man was afraid.
His actions with a constant conquest shine,
From Villa-Viciosa to the Rhine.
France, Flanders, Germany, his fame confess,
And all the world was fond of him, but us.
Our turn first served, we grudged him the command:
Witness the grateful temper of the land.

We blame the King that he relies too much
On strangers, Germans, Hugonots, and Dutch,
And seldom does his great affairs of state
To English counsellors communicate.
The fact might very well be answered thus:
He has so often been betrayed by us,
He must have been a madman to rely
On English Godolphin's fidelity.
For laying other arguments aside,
This thought might mortify our English pride,
That foreigners have faithfully obeyed him,
And none but Englishmen have e'er betrayed him.
They have our ships and merchants bought and sold,
And bartered English blood for foreign gold.
First to the French they sold our Turkey fleet,
And injured Talmarsh next at Camaret.
The King himself is sheltered from their snares,
Not by his merit, but the crown he wears.
Experience tells us 'tis the English way
Their benefactors always to betray.

And lest examples should be too remote,
A modern magistrate of famous note
Shall give you his own character by rote.
I'll make it out, deny it he that can,
His worship is a true-born Englishman,
In all the latitude of that empty word,
By modern acceptations understood.
The parish books his great descent record,
And now he hopes ere long to be a lord.
And truly, as things go, it would be pity
But such as he should represent the City:
While robbery for burnt-offering he brings,
And gives to God what he has stole from kings:
Great monuments of charity he raises,
And good St. Magnus whistles out his praises.
To City gaols he grants a jubilee,
And hires huzzas from his own Mobilee.[1]
Lately he wore the golden chain and gown,
With which equipped, he thus harangued the town.

[1] "Mobile," applied to the moveable, unstable populace, was first abridged to "mob" in Charles the Second's time.

HIS FINE SPEECH, ETC.

With clouted iron shoes and sheep-skin breeches,
More rags than manners, and more dirt than riches;
From driving cows and calves to Layton Market,
While of my greatness there appeared no spark yet,
Behold I come, to let you see the pride
With which exalted beggars always ride.

Born to the needful labours of the plough,
The cart-whip graced me, as the chain does now.
Nature and Fate, in doubt what course to take,
Whether I should a lord or plough-boy make,
Kindly at last resolved they would promote me,
And first a knave, and then a knight, they vote me.

What Fate appointed, Nature did prepare,
And furnished me with an exceeding care,
To fit me for what they designed to have me;
And every gift, but honesty, they gave me.

And thus equipped, to this proud town I came,
In quest of bread, and not in quest of fame.
Blind to my future fate, a humble boy,
Free from the guilt and glory I enjoy,
The hopes which my ambition entertained
Were in the name of foot-boy all contained.
The greatest heights from small beginnings rise;
The gods were great on earth before they reached the skies.

B—well, the generous temper of whose mind
Was ever to be bountiful inclined,
Whether by his ill-fate or fancy led,
First took me up, and furnished me with bread.
The little services he put me to
Seemed labours, rather than were truly so.
But always my advancement he designed,
For 'twas his very nature to be kind.
Large was his soul, his temper ever free;
The best of masters and of men to me.
And I, who was before decreed by Fate
To be made infamous as well as great,
With an obsequious diligence obeyed him,
Till trusted with his all, and then betrayed him.

All his past kindnesses I trampled on,
Ruined his fortunes to erect my own.
So vipers in the bosom bred, begin
To hiss at that hand first which took them in.

With eager treachery I his fall pursued,
And my first trophies were Ingratitude.

Ingratitude, the worst of human wit,
The basest action mankind can commit;
Which, like the sin against the Holy Ghost,
Has least of honour, and of guilt the most;
Distinguished from all other crimes by this,
That 'tis a crime which no man will confess.
That sin alone, which should not be forgiven
On earth, although perhaps it may in Heaven.

Thus my first benefactor I o'erthrew;
And how should I be to a second true?
The public trusts came next into my care,
And I to use them scurvily prepare.
My needy sovereign lord I played upon,
And lent him many a thousand of his own;
For which great interests I took care to charge,
And so my ill-got wealth became so large.

My predecessor, Judas, was a fool,
Fitter to have been whipped and sent to school
Than sell a Saviour. Had I been at hand,
His Master had not been so cheap trepanned;
I would have made the eager Jews have found,
For forty pieces, thirty thousand pound.

My Cousin, Ziba, of immortal fame,
(Ziba and I shall never want a name),
First-born of treason, nobly did advance
His master's fall for his inheritance,
By whose keen arts old David first began
To break his sacred oath to Jonathan:
The good old king, 'tis thought, was very loth
To break his word, and therefore broke his oath.
Ziba's a traitor of some quality,
Yet Ziba might have been informed by me:
Had I been there, he ne'er had been content
With half the estate, nor half the government.

In our late revolution 'twas thought strange
That I, of all mankind, should like the change;
But they who wondered at it never knew
That in it I did my old game pursue;
Nor had they heard of twenty thousand pound,
Which never yet was lost, nor ne'er was found.

Thus all things in their turn to sale I bring,
God and my master first, and then the King;
Till, by successful villanies made bold,
I thought to turn the nation into gold;
And so to forgery my hand I bent,
Not doubting I could gull the Government;
But there was ruffled by the Parliament.
And if I 'scaped the unhappy tree to climb,
'Twas want of law, and not for want of crime.

But my old friend,[1] who printed in my face
A needful competence of English brass,
Having more business yet for me to do,
And loth to lose his trusty servant so,
Managed the matter with such art and skill,
As saved his hero and threw out the bill.

[1] The Devil.—[D.F.]

And now I'm graced with unexpected honours,
For which I'll certainly abuse the donors.
Knighted, and made a tribune of the people,
Whose laws and properties I'm like to keep well;
The custos rotulorum of the City,
And captain of the guards of their banditti.
Surrounded by my catchpoles, I declare
Against the needy debtor open war;
I hang poor thieves for stealing of your pelf,
And suffer none to rob you but myself.

The King commanded me to help reform ye,
And how I'll do't, Miss shall inform ye.
I keep the best seraglio in the nation,
And hope in time to bring it into fashion.
For this my praise is sung by every bard,
For which Bridewell would be a just reward.
In print my panegyrics fill the streets,
And hired gaol-birds their huzzas repeat.
Some charities contrived to make a show,
Have taught the needy rabble to do so,
Whose empty noise is a mechanic fame,
Since for Sir Belzebub they'd do the same.

THE CONCLUSION

Then let us boast of ancestors no more,

Or deeds of heroes done in days of yore,
In latent records of the ages past,
Behind the rear of time, in long oblivion placed.
For if our virtues must in lines descend,
The merit with the families would end,
And intermixtures would most fatal grow;
For vice would be hereditary too;
The tainted blood would of necessity
In voluntary wickedness convey.

Vice, like ill-nature, for an age or two
May seem a generation to pursue;
But virtue seldom does regard the breed;
Fools do the wise, and wise men fools succeed.
What is't to us what ancestors we had?
If good, what better? or what worse, if bad?
Examples are for imitation set,
Yet all men follow virtue with regret.

Could but our ancestors retrieve the fate,
And see their offspring thus degenerate;
How we contend for birth and names unknown,
And build on their past actions, not our own;
They'd cancel records, and their tombs deface,
And openly disown the vile degenerate race:
For fame of families is all a cheat,
'Tis personal virtue only makes us great.

Daniel Defoe – A Short Biography

Daniel Foe was born around 1660 in Fore Street in the parish of St. Giles Cripplegate in London.

The aristocratic-sounding 'De' was added to his name to create 'Defoe'. On occasion he was prone to claim descent from the family of De Beau Faux.

His father, James Foe, was a prosperous tallow chandler and a member of the Worshipful Company of Butchers and, with Defoe's mother, Annie, Presbyterian dissenters.

Defoe has been born into a time that was rich in dramatic history. In 1665, 70,000 were killed by the Great Plague of London. The following year the Great Fire of London destroyed much of mediaeval London. The Defoe house was one of the few to survive.

In 1667, a third calamity beset London when a Dutch fleet sailed up the Medway via the River Thames and attacked the town of Chatham, as well as destroying much of the British fleet.

By the time Defoe was aged ten accounts suggest his mother, Annie, had died.

Defoe's education began at James Fisher's boarding school in Pixham Lane in Dorking, Surrey. By 14 he was attending a dissenting academy at Newington Green in London run by Charles Morton, and he is then believed to have attended the Newington Green Unitarian Church. During this period, the English government persecuted those who chose to worship outside the Church of England.

Defoe entered the world of business as a general merchant, dealing at different times in hosiery, general woollen goods and wine. His ambitions were great and he was able to buy a country estate, a ship as well as civets, though he was rarely out of debt. (The civet produces an odorous secretion for the purpose of marking out their territory. Diluted, after some time, the odor of civet secretion, normally strong and repulsive, becomes pleasant with animalistic-musk nuance. The animals are kept in cages in order to be able to collect the secretions and thence perfume).

In 1684, Defoe married Mary Tuffley, the daughter of a London merchant, and received a dowry of £3,700 – a huge amount by the standards of the day. With his debts and political difficulties, the marriage may have been troubled, but it lasted 50 years.

In 1685, Defoe joined the ill-fated Monmouth Rebellion but gained a pardon, by which he escaped the Bloody Assizes of the notorious Judge George Jeffreys.

The Glorious Revolution brought Queen Mary and her husband William III to the crown in 1688, and Defoe became one of William's close allies and a secret agent. Some of the new Government policies led to conflict with France, thus damaging many of Defoe's trade relationships.

In 1692, Defoe was arrested for debts of £700 and his civets were taken away. His actual debts are thought to have been nearer £17,000. His laments were loud and he always sided with debtors, but there is evidence that his financial dealings were always above board.

With a wife and seven children to support it was essential that his release was quickly enabled. He achieved this and accounts then suggest he travelled to Europe and Scotland, perhaps to re-establish some business relationships and to trade wine.

By 1695, he was back in England, serving as a "commissioner of the glass duty", and responsible for collecting the tax on bottles. The following year, 1696, he ran a tile and brick factory in what is now Tilbury in Essex and the family lived in the parish of Chadwell St Mary.

Defoe's first notable publication was not one of his great fiction works but a series of proposals for social and economic improvements, a subject for which he had a keen eye and many ideas. An Essay upon Projects was published in 1697.

His most successful poem, The True-Born Englishman (1701), defended the king against the perceived xenophobia of his enemies, satirising the English claim to racial purity. That same year Defoe presented the Legion's Memorial to the Speaker of the House of Commons and later his employer, Robert Harley, flanked by a guard of sixteen gentlemen of quality. It demanded the release of the Kentish petitioners, who had asked Parliament to support the king in an imminent war against France.

In 1702 the death of William III once more created a political crisis. Queen Anne immediately began an attack against Non-conformists. Defoe was one of the first targets. His pamphleteering and political activities quickly resulted in his arrest. This seemed mainly predicated on his December 1702 pamphlet; The Shortest-Way with the Dissenters; Or, Proposals for the Establishment of the Church, which argued for their extermination. In it, he ruthlessly satirised both the High church Tories and those Dissenters who hypocritically practised so-called "occasional conformity". Although it was published anonymously, the Defoe's authorship was quickly unmasked and he was arrested and charged with seditious libel. In fact, Defoe's ironic writing had been misinterpreted, but, alas for him, his trial was to be at the Old bailey in front of the sadistic judge Salathiel Lovell.

Lovell sentenced him to a punitive fine of 200 marks, to public humiliation in a pillory at Charing Cross and an indeterminate length of imprisonment at the Queen's pleasure which would cease only on payment of the enormous fine.

This was an awful moment for Defoe. After his three days in the pillory, he was imprisoned at Newgate.

In despair, he wrote to William Paterson, the London Scot and founder of the Bank of England and who was in the confidence of Robert Harley, 1st Earl of Oxford and Earl Mortimer, a leading minister and spymaster in the English Government. Harley arranged Defoe's release, in 1703, in exchange for Defoe's co-operation as an intelligence agent for the Tories. In exchange for such co-operation with the rival political side, Harley paid some of Defoe's very large outstanding debts, which greatly improved his financial situation.

With his release from Newgate Defoe had, within a few days, witnessed the Great Storm of November 26th, 1703. It caused immense damage to an area from London to Bristol, uprooting millions of trees, and claiming the lives of over 8,000 people, mostly at sea. This became the subject of The Storm (1704), which included many eye-witness accounts and is regarded as one of the world's first examples of modern journalism.

In the same year, he set up his periodical A Review of the Affairs of France which supported the Harley Ministry, and chronicled the events of the War of the Spanish Succession (1702–1714). The Review initially ran weekly but was soon being printed three times a week. Defoe wrote most of the articles himself and although in effect the Review was a Government publication Defoe was enthusiastic and energetic as ever.

Harley was ousted from the ministry in 1708, but Defoe continued writing the Review to support a new master, Godolphin, then again to support Harley and his return in the Tory ministry of 1710–1714. The Tories fell from power with the death of Queen Anne, but Defoe continued his work, now for the Whig government, writing 'Tory' pamphlets that undermined the Tory point of view.

Not all of Defoe's pamphlet writing was political. One pamphlet was originally published anonymously, entitled 'A True Relation of the Apparition of One Mrs. Veal the Next Day after her Death to One Mrs. Bargrave at Canterbury the 8th of September, 1705.' It deals with the crossover between the spiritual and physical realms and describes Mrs. Bargrave's encounter with her old friend Mrs. Veal after she had died.

In 1709, Defoe authored a rather lengthy book entitled The History of the Union of Great Britain. The book attempts to explain the facts leading up to the Act of Union 1707, dating all the way back to December 6th, 1604 when King James was presented with a proposal for unification. (It should be remembered that since the death of Queen Elizabeth England and Scotland, although separate kingdoms, had a common monarch; known as James I of England and as James VI of Scotland. The act now brought the two countries into one; Great Britain.

Part of Defoe's duties as a Government spokesman and spy was the relaying of the Governments view to the public. He thought that his work on the Review would end the threat from the north and gain for the Treasury an "inexhaustible treasury of men", a valuable new market increasing the power of England, clearly the senior partner in the Union. In September 1706, Harley ordered Defoe to Edinburgh to do everything he could to secure loyalty to the Treaty of Union. Defoe was conscious of the risk he was taking. His reports were often vivid descriptions of violent demonstrations against the Union. "A Scots rabble is the worst of its kind", he reported.

Defoe was a Presbyterian who had suffered in England for his convictions, and as such he was accepted as an adviser to the General Assembly of the Church of Scotland and committees of the Parliament of Scotland with little problem.

Defoe received little in the way of reward or recognition from his pay-masters or the government. However, like any good writer, the experiences would be filed away for later use. The Scottish experience was helpful when he came to write his Tour Thro' the Whole Island of Great Britain, published in 1726.

Defoe continued to keep up a wide and varied output including in his apologia Appeal to Honour and Justice (1715), a defence of his part in Harley's Tory ministry (1710–14), The Family Instructor (1715), a conduct manual on religious duty; Minutes of the Negotiations of Monsr. Mesnager (1717), in which he impersonates Nicolas Mesnager, who negotiated the Treaty of Utrecht (1713); and A Continuation of the Letters Writ by a Turkish Spy (1718), a satire of European politics and religion, written by Defoe in the guise of a Muslim in Paris.

From this point Defoe would now enter a period of writing that would cement his place in the canon of English fiction. From 1719 to 1724, Defoe published the novels for which he is now world-famous including Robinson Crusoe in 1719 and Moll Flanders in 1724 amongst many others.

In the final decade of his life, he also wrote conduct manuals, including Religious Courtship (1722), The Complete English Tradesman (1726) and The New Family Instructor (1727).

Defoe seemed to have a natural knack of writing across a wide range of subjects and from a number of points of view. He published on the breakdown of the social order; The Great Law of Subordination Considered (1724) and Everybody's Business is Nobody's Business (1725), together with works on the supernatural; The Political History of the Devil (1726), A System of Magick (1727) and An Essay on the History and Reality of Apparitions (1727). His works on foreign travel and trade include A General History of Discoveries and Improvements (1727) and Atlas Maritimus and Commercialis (1728). Perhaps his greatest achievement is the magisterial A Tour Thro' the Whole Island of Great Britain (1724–27), which provided a panoramic survey of British trade on the eve of the Industrial Revolution.

Published in 1726, The Complete English Tradesman is a late example of Defoe's political and social work. He discusses the role of the tradesman in England in comparison to those abroad, arguing that the British system of trade is far superior. He also states that trade is the backbone of the British economy: "estate's a pond, but trade's a spring."

Defoe was obviously keenly aware of both political and economic structures. Trade, Defoe argues, is a much better vehicle for social and economic change than war. He states that through imperialism and trade expansion the British empire is able to "increase commerce at home" through job creation and increased consumption. This increased consumption, by laws of supply and demand, increases production which in turn raises wages for the poor therefore lifting part of British society further out of poverty.

Daniel Defoe died on April 24th, 1731. Some accounts say that it was whilst hiding from his creditors. Indeed, Defoe was known to enjoy walking on a Sunday when, legally, it was the only day of the week when he could not be legally pestered about his bills. The cause of his death was given as lethargy, but it is thought it was more probably a stroke.

He was interred in Bunhill Fields, London. A monument was erected to his memory there in 1870.

There are various suggestions as to the number of works in Defoe's literary output. Certainly, no less than 200 separate pieces but accounts suggest perhaps as many as 500 which seems, even for so prolific a writer as Defoe, rather too generous but perhaps is in keeping with the extravagance of his life.

Daniel Defoe – A Concise Bibliography

Defoe wrote an immense amount of works. Some were under pseudonyms or anonymously and others may merely have been attributed to him. The list below is by no means exhaustive but is certainly illustrative of both his range and scope.

Novels
Robinson Crusoe (1719)
The Farther Adventures of Robinson Crusoe (1719)
Serious Reflections During the Life and Surprising Adventures of Robinson Crusoe; With His Vision of the Angelic World (1720)
Captain Singleton (1720)
Memoirs of a Cavalier (1720)
A Journal of the Plague Year (1722)
Colonel Jack (1722)
Moll Flanders (1722)
Roxana: The Fortunate Mistress (1724)
Memoirs of a Cavalier: A Military Journal of the Wars in Germany, and the Wars in England.: From the Year 1632 to the Year 1648 (1724)
A New Voyage Round the World (1725)
Military Memoirs of Capt. George Carleton (1728)
A General History of the Pyrates, From their First Rise and Settlement in the Island of Providence, to the Present Time (1724)
The History of the Pyrates (1728)
Of Captain Misson and his Crew (1728)

Essays, Satires & Other Pieces

An Essay Upon Projects (1697)
The Shortest Way with the Dissenters (1702)
New Test of Church of England's Loyalty (1702)
Ode to the Athenian Society (1703)
Enquiry into Acgill's General Translation (1703)
The Storm– a description of the worst storm to hit Britain in recorded times, which includes eyewitness accounts. (1704)
The Great Law of Subordination Consider'd (1704)
Layman's Sermon on the Late Storm (1704)
Elegy on Author of 'True–Born Englishman,' (1704)
Hymn to Victory (1704)
An Essay on the Regulation of the Press (1704)
Giving Alms No Charity (1704)
The Consolidator or, Memoirs of Sundry Transactions from the World in the Moon (1705)
A True Relation of the Apparition of Mrs. Veal (1706)
Sermon on the Filling-up of Dr. Burgess's Meeting-house (1706)
History of the Union of Great Britain (1709)
Atalantis Major (1711)
A Short narrative of the Life and Actions of His Grace John, Duke of Marlborough (1711)
A Seasonable Warning and Caution Against the Insinuations of Papists and Jacobites in Favour of the Pretender (1712)
Short Enquiry into a Late Duel (1713)
A General History of Trade (1713)
An Answer to a Question That Nobody Thinks of, VIZ. But What if the Queen should die? (1713)
Reasons Against the Succession of the House of Hanover with an Enquiry How far the Abdication of King James, Supposing it to be Legal, Ought to Affect the Person of the Pretender (1713)
Wars of Charles III. (1715)
The Family Instructor (1715)
Hymn to the Mob (1715)
The Family Instructor (1715)
An Appeal to Honour and Justice, Though It Be of His Worst Enemies: Being A True Account of His Conduct in Public Affairs (1715)
A Friendly Epistle by Way of Reproof from one of the People Called Quakers, to T. B., a Dealer in Many Words (1715)
Memoirs of the Church of Scotland (1717)
Life and Death of Count Patkul (1717)
Memoirs of the Church of Scotland (1717)
Memoirs of Major Alexander Ramkins (1718)
Memoirs of Duke of Shrewsbury (1718)
Memoirs of Daniel Williams (1718)
A Vindication of the Press (1718)
Dickory Cronke: The Dumb Philosopher: or, Great Britain's Wonder (1719)
The King of Pirates (Capt. Avery) (1719)
Life of Baron de Goertz (1719)
Life and Adventures of Duncan Campbell (1720)
Mr. Campbell's Pacquet (1720)
The Supernatural Philosopher; or, The Mysteries of Magick (1720)
Due Preparations for the Plague (1722)

Life of Cartouche (1722)
Religious Courtship (1722)
History of Peter the Great (1723)
The Highland Rogue (Rob Roy) (1723)
Narrative of Murders at Calais (1724)
The History of The Remarkable Life of John Sheppard (1724)
A Narrative of All The Robberies, Escapes, &c. of John Sheppard (1724)
A Tour Thro' the Whole Island of Great Britain, Divided into Circuits or Journies (1724–1727)
The Great Law of Subordination; or, the Insolence and Insufferable Behaviour of Servants in England (1724)
Account of Jonathan Wild (1725)
Account of John Gow (1725)
Every-body's Business, Is No-body's Business (1725)
The Complete English Tradesman (1725; volume II, 1727)
The Friendly Demon (1726)
Mere Nature Delineated (Peter the Wild Boy) (1726)
Essay upon Literature and the Original of Letters (1726)
History of Discoveries (1726–7)
A System of Magic (1726)
The Protestant Monastery (1726)
The Political History of the Devil (1726)
An Essay Upon Literature (1726)
Mere Nature Delineated (1726)
Conjugal Lewdness (1727)
Treatise concerning Use and Abuse of Marriage (1727)
Secrets of Invisible World Discovered; or, History and Reality of Apparitions (1727)
Parochial Tyranny (1727)
A New Family Instructor (1728)
Augusta Triumphans: or, The Way to Make London the Most Flourishing City in the Universe (1728)
Plan of English Commerce (1728)
Second Thoughts are Best (on Street Robberies) (1728)
Street Robberies Considered (1728)
A Plan of the English Commerce (1728)
Humble Proposal to People of England for Increase of Trade, &c. (1729)
Preface to R. Dodsley's Poem 'Servitude' (1729)
Effectual Scheme for Preventing Street Robberies (1731)

Works in Verse
A New Discovery of an Old Intreague (1691)
Character of Dr. Samuel Annesley (1697)
The Pacificator (1700)
The True-Born Englishman: A Satyr (1701)
Reformation of Manners (1702)
The Mock Mourners (1702)
More Reformation (1703)
Hymn to the Pillory (1703)
The Dyet of Poland (1705)

Jure Divino. A Satyr in 12 books. (1706)
Caledonia (1706)
Translation of Du Fresnoy's "Compleat Art of Painting" (1720)

www.ingramcontent.com/pod-product-compliance
Lightning Source LLC
Chambersburg PA
CBHW071958060426
42444CB00043B/2597